COCKNEY

D1080958

DIALECT

A Selection of Cockney
Words and Anecdotes

by
Kate Sanderson

BRADWELL
BOOKS

Published by Bradwell Books
9 Orgreave Close Sheffield S13 9NP
Email: books@bradwellbooks.co.uk

British Library Cataloguing in Publication Data:
a catalogue record for this book is available
from the British Library.

1st Edition

ISBN: 9781902674643

Print: Gomer Press, Llandysul, Ceredigion SA44 4JL

Design by: Andrew Caffrey

Photograph Credits: Blind Beggar Pub, Robert Milligan,
Tubby Isaac's Jellied Eels Stall, Twinings, West India Quay
Warehouses, William Booth © C. Sanderson
All other photographs © Tower Hamlets Local History
Library and Archives

Flag on front cover:
shutterstock_137200574 Copyright Bojan Pavlukovic

INTRODUCTION

Well then, me ol' Chinas, this secret language may have originated not only from the costermongers but also from smugglers and seamen as well as from dubious places such as the opium dens of Limehouse. All of these people wished to be understood only by those in the know, and not by the authorities or their customers! Before rhyming slang, words were often pronounced backwards and even children were fluent in this. It may have been around the 1840s when Cockney rhyming slang began to be used by costermongers in the East End. There is something romantic about rhymes, and seamen picked up on it, spreading its usage to other ports; my grandfather would come out with these same rhymes when he worked at the docks in Glasgow.

However, it is much more complicated than that. It may be all right for outsiders to understand 'sausage 'n' mash' to mean cash, but if only the first word is used and not the rhyming word, then it is more difficult to work out the meaning, as when 'not having a sausage' means broke.

Walking along Whitechapel Road these days, it is rare to hear a Cockney voice amongst the market traders and their customers. A cabbie has assured me that many Cockneys have moved away to Essex, and Romford Market is where you will find them. Having said that, I have met many people from the East End who have kindly shared their memories with me and would live nowhere else and love this ever-changing, vibrant, friendly part of London.

A recent survey on Cockney rhyming slang by the Museum of London Docklands showed that seven out of ten people think that it is dying out or fading. On the positive side, two-thirds think that it is crucial to London's identity. So here is your chance to 'ave a butcher's and get rabbitin'.

Kate Sanderson

Schneider's Tailor Workshop in Durward Street, 1916

A

Abaht – about

Abbott's Priory – King's Bench Prison

Abergavenny – penny

Acker Bilk – milk

Adam 'n' Eve – believe

Adrian Mole – dole

Airs 'n' graces – braces

A la mode – code

Alan Whicker's – knickers

Alligator – later

Ally Pally – Alexandra Palace

Almond Rocks – socks – Almond Rocks were a Victorian almond biscuit, possibly of Indian origin

Apple core – score, twenty

Apple peeling – feeling

Apple pips – lips

Apple tart – heart

Apples 'n' pears – stairs

Apples 'n' rice – nice

April fools – football pools

April showers – flowers

Aristotle – bottle

Army 'n' Navy – gravy

Artful Dodger – lodger

Attila – 2:1 university degree – refers to Atilla the Hun, not known for academic study

Aunty Lou – flu

B

Babbling brook – cook, sometimes crook

Backseat driver – skiver

Bacon rind – blind

Bacon 'n' eggs – legs

Baden-Powell – trowel – Baden-Powell was the founder of the scout movement

Bag of sand – a grand, £1,000

Baked beans – jeans

Baker's dozen – cousin

Ball of fat – cat

Bangers 'n' mash – cash

Barnet Fair – hair

Barney Rubble – trouble, fight, violent argument – Barney Rubble is a character in "The Flintstones"

Bath bun – son, sun

Battle cruiser – boozer, public house

Battle of the Nile – tile, hat

Baze, the – Bayswater Road

Beano – beanfeast, a celebratory dinner, works outing

Bedlam – pandemonium – Bethlem Royal Hospital, a lunatic asylum, moved from Moorfields to St George's Fields in 1815 and remained there until the 1930s

Beecham's pill – hill, Old Bill (police) – Beecham's pills were a cure for just about everything!

Beehive – five

Bees 'n' honey – money

Beetles 'n' ants – underpants

Bengal Lancer – chancer

Berk – fool, unwise person, rhymes with Berkeley Hunt

Bernard Miles – piles, haemorrhoids

Big dippers – slippers

Bill 'n' Ben – ten – from the children's TV series "The Flower Pot Men"

Bill 'n' Benner – tenner, ten pound note

Billy Bunter – punter

Billy Button – mutton

Bin lid – quid, one pound

Bird lime – time, as in prison sentence

Birds and bees – knees

Bladder of lard – card, Scotland Yard

Blinder – amazing, great

Boat race – face

Bobby Moore – door

Bonnie and Clyde – snide

Bo-peep – sleep

Bonkers – slightly crazy

Boracic lint – skint, broke, penniless

Bottle 'n' glass – arse, backside

Bottle of porter – daughter – porter is a type of beer

Bottle of sauce – horse

Bottle of scent – bent, corrupt or dodgy

Bovver – bother

Bowler hat – rat

Bow 'n' arrow – barrow, sparrow

Bow 'n' quiver – liver

Bowl the hoop – soup

Box of toys – noise

Brass tacks – basic facts

Bread 'n' butter – gutter, broke, penniless

Bread 'n' cheese – sneeze

Bread 'n' honey – money

Brahms 'n' Liszt – pissed, drunk

Brandy butter – nutter, crazy person

Bricks 'n' mortar – daughter

Bright 'n' breezy – easy, easy going

Brighton Rock – dock, as in a courtroom

Bristol 'n' West – chest

Britneys – beers, rhymes with Britney Speers

Brixton briefcase – ghetto-blaster, a portable radio

Brixton riot – diet

Brown bread – dead

Brussels sprout – Boy Scout
Bubble bath – laugh
Bubble 'n' squeak – speak, week
Buck 'n' doe – snow
Bucket 'n' pail – jail, prison
Bull 'n' cow – row, loud disagreement
Bullock's horn – pawn
Bull's eye – £50
Bunny – talk, as in rabbit 'n' pork
Burnt cinder – window – pronounced 'winda'
Burton-on-Trent – rent
Bushel 'n' peck – neck
Bushey Park – lark, mischief
Butcher's hook – look

C

Cain 'n' Abel – table
Calcutta – butter
Canoes – shoes
Cape Horn – corn
Captain Cook – book
Cash 'n' carry – marry
Chalk Farm – arm
Charlie Sheen – screen
Cherry 'og – dog

Cherry ripe – pipe

Chew the fat – chat, gossip idly

Chicken 'n' rice – nice

China plate – mate, friend

Chocolate fudge – judge

Chopsticks – six

Chovey – travelling shop

Clink – prison

Clippies – female bus conductors who clipped tickets

Clobber – clothes

Clothes pegs – legs

Coach 'n' badge – cadge

Coal 'n' coke – broke, no cash, skint

Cock 'n' hen – ten

Cock linnet – minute

Cockroach – coach

Cock sparrow – barrow, mate

Coffee 'n' tea – sea

Conan Doyle – boil

Country cousin – dozen

Cow 'n' kisses – missus, wife

Cream-crackered – knackered, exhausted

Currant bun – son

Currant cakes – the shakes, delirium tremens

Custard 'n' jelly – telly, television

Cuts 'n' scratches – matches

D

Daisy roots – boots
Dancing bears – stairs
Darby 'n' Joan – alone or a loan
Davy Crockett – pocket
Deep fat fryer – liar
Deep sea diver – fiver, £5 note
Derry 'n' Tom – bomb
Desmond – 2:2, lower second class honours degree – from
Archbishop Desmond Tutu
Dicky bird – word
Dicky Dirt – shirt
Dig in the grave – shave
Ding-dong – song, sing-song
Doctor Crippen – dripping, fat from a meat roast
Dog 'n' bone – telephone
Donald Duck – luck
Donkey's ears – years
Dough – money
Duchess – wife, rhymes with Duchess of Fife
Duck 'n' dive – skive
Duke of Kent – rent
Duke of York – pork, cork, fork
Dunnit – doesn't it, often used at the end of a sentence
Dutch plate – mate

E

Eiffel Tower – shower
Eighteen pence – sense, fence as in garden
Epsom races – braces
Errol Flynns – binns, binoculars
Everton toffee – coffee

F

Feather 'n' flip – kip, nap, sleep
Field of wheat – street
Fine 'n' dandy – brandy
Fink – think
Firm, The – an organised gang of criminals
Fisherman's daughter – water
Fiver – five-pound note
Flash – confident and overdressed
Fleas 'n' ants – pants
Fleet Street – sheet
Flowery dell – cell in a prison
Fly-by-nights – tights
Fore and aft – daft
France 'n' Spain – rain, abbreviated to 'Frarny'
Friar Tuck – luck
Fridge freezer – geezer

Frog 'n' toad – road
Fruit Gum – chum
Frying pan – old man, husband

G

Gaff – house, place to stay
Gammon rasher – smasher, someone attractive
Gander – look, to look in detail
Garden gate – eight, magistrate
Gates of heaven – seven
Gates of Rome – home
Gawdelpus – God help us
Gedoudovit – get out of it
Glasgow Rangers – strangers
George Raft – daft, crazy
Gold watch – Scotch whisky
Goose's neck – cheque
Grand – £1,000
Greengages – wages – the old British pound note was
printed in green ink
Grey mare – fair
Gypsy's warning – morning

H

Haddock 'n' bloater – motor

Hairy muff – fair enough

Half-inch – pinch, steal

Half-ouncer – bouncer

Ha'penny dip – ship

Ham shanks – Yanks, Americans

Ham 'n' eggs – legs

Hampstead Heath – teeth

Harpers 'n' Queens – jeans

Harry Lime – time

Harry Tate – late

Hat 'n' feather – weather

Harvey Nichols – pickles

Heap of coke – bloke, man

Hedge 'n' ditch – pitch, market stall

Hen 'n' fox – box

Highland fling – ring

Hit 'n' miss – kiss

Hokey-Cokey – Cockney song and dance

Holy friar – liar

Holy Ghost – toast; or racecourse winning post

Horn of plenty – twenty

Horse 'n' carriage – garage

Horse 'n' cart – heart

Horse 'n' trough – cough
House to let – bet
Huckleberry Finn – PIN, as used in a cash machine

I

Inky blue – flu
Inky smudge – judge
Innit – isn't it – often used at the end of sentences

J

Jackanory – story
Jack the Lad – bad
Jack the Rippers – slippers, kippers
Jack's alive – five
Jack Sprat – brat
Jam jar – car
Jam roll – parole, dole
Jam tart – heart, sweetheart
Jamaica rum – thumb
Jar of jam – tram, pram
Jellied eels – wheels, car
Jenny Lee – key
Jeremiah – fire
Jim Skinner – dinner

Joan of Arc – park
Joanna – piano – pronounced 'pianah'
Joe Baxi – taxi
Joe Blake – steak
Joe Hook – crook
Judi Dench – stench
Jumbo jet – bet

K

Kate Carney – army
Kate 'n' Sidney – steak and kidney
Kidney punch – lunch
Kingdom come – bum, bottom
King Lear's – ears
Knees up – party
Knock on the door – four

L

Lady from Bristol – pistol
Lady Godiva – fiver, five-pound note
Lally – leg
Lambeth Walk – Cockney song and dance; chalk as used on the tip of a snooker cue
Laugh 'n' joke – smoke

Laugh 'n' titter – bitter, beer

Left in the lurch – church

Leggit – run away as fast as possible

Lemon 'n' lime – crime

Lemon squash – wash

Lemon squeezer – geezer, person

Lemon squeezy – easy

Lemonade – spade

Life 'n' death – breath

Light 'n' dark – park

Light of my life – wife

Lillian Gish – fish

Linen draper – newspaper

Lion's roar – snore

Liquor – green parsley sauce served with jellied eels and pie 'n' mash

Loaf of bread – head

Lolly – money

London fog – dog

Long 'n' linger – finger

Lord, love a duck! – That's a surprise!

Lord Mayor – swear

Lorna Doone – spoon

Lost 'n' found – pound

Love 'n' kisses – Missus, wife

Lovely jubbly! – money, wealth, fantastic – Jubbly was an orange drink in a pyramid-shaped wax carton, sometimes served frozen

Lucy Locket – pocket

M

Macaroni – pony, £25

Malarkey – nonsense

Manhole cover – brother

Max Miller – pillar

Maxwell House – mouse

Me and you – two, menu

Mickey Mouse – house

Millwall Reserves – nerves

Mince pies – eyes

Mix 'n' muddle – cuddle

Moby Dick – sick

Mockney – a mixture of 'cockney' and 'mock', an imitation of cockney speech

Monkey – £500, thought to originate from Indian five hundred rupee notes which portrayed a monkey

Monkey's tail – nail

Moolah – money

Mother Brown – town

Mother Hubbard – cupboard

Mother-in-law – saw

Mother of mine – nine

Mother of Pearl – girl
Mother's pride – bride
Mother's ruin – gin
Mouldies – small change – children running alongside coaches and wedding cars would shout 'Chuck out your mouldies!'
Mud Island – Southend-on-Sea
Mutt 'n' Jeff – deaf
Mystic Megs – legs

N

Nark it – stop it
Near 'n' far – bar, pub
Needle 'n' pin – thin
Needle 'n' thread – bread
Nelson Eddy's – readies, cash
Nelson Mandela – Stella Artois beer
Nervous wreck – cheque
Newington Butts – guts
Nick – prison; to steal
Nifty – smart, stylish, fifty
Nigel Mansell – cancelled
Nipper – small child
Nippies – waitresses in Lyons' Corner House restaurants, the last one closed in 1977

Noah's Ark – nark, police informer
North 'n' south – mouth
Not a sausage – no money – sausage 'n' mash being cash
Not on your Nellie – no way
Nuffink – nothing
Number nine – Fleet Prison

O

Ocean wave – shave
Oily rag – fag, cigarette
Oliver Twist – fist
Ones 'n' twos – shoes
Overcoat maker – undertaker
Oxford scholar – US Dollar
Oxo Cube – tube, London Underground

P

Pair of kippers – slippers
Paraffin lamp – tramp
Pat and Mick – sick
Peas in the pot – hot
Peashooter – hooter, nose
Peckham Rye – tie
Pen 'n' ink – stink, smell

Penny bun – one

Peter Pan – van

Piccadilly – silly, abbreviated to 'picca'

Piccadilly Percy – mercy

Pie 'n' liquor – vicar

Pie 'n' mash – flash

Pig's ear – beer

Pill Avenue – Harley Street

Pitch 'n' toss – boss

Plates of meat – feet

Pleasure 'n' pain – rain

Plonk or **Plinkety plonk** – wine

Polly Parrots – carrots

Pony – twenty-five pounds

Pop – pawn

Poppy – money

Pork pies – lies

Pot 'n' pan – old man, husband

Pots 'n' dishes – wishes

Pride 'n' joy – boy

Proppa – proper

Pure – dog poo

Q

Queen of the Costermongers – Mary Robinson, vendor of meat for cats who died in 1884

R

Rabbit 'n' pork – talk

Rag 'n' bone – throne, toilet

Raquel Welch – belch

Raspberry tart – fart

Rats 'n' mice – dice

Rawalpindi – windy

Razor – blazer

Reads 'n' writes – fights

Reels of cotton – rotten

Ribbon 'n' curl – girl

Richard Todd – cod

River Ouse – booze, alcoholic drink

Roast pork – fork

Rock 'n' boulder – shoulder

Rock 'n' roll – dole

Rocking horse – sauce

Roman candles – sandals

Ronnie Biggs – digs, lodgings, rented accommodation

Rory O'Moore – floor

Rosie Lee – tea

Royal Mail – jail

Rub-a-dub – pub

Ruby Murray – curry

Ruby rose – nose

Ruck – a fight
Rupert Bears – shares – Rupert Bear is a cartoon strip character

S

Salmon 'n' trout – gout
Saucepan lid – kid, child
Sausage 'n' mash – cash
Sausage roll – dole, unemployment benefit
Saveloy – the Savoy Hotel
Scapa Flow – go
Scarper – to run away quickly, make a fast exit
Scooby Doo – clue
Semolina – cleaner
Sexton Blake – cake
Shake 'n' shiver – river
Shepherd's pie – sky
Sherbert dip – tip
Ship in full sail – ale, beer
Shovel 'n' broom – room
Shovel 'n' pick – nick, prison
Shyme – shame
Silver spoon – moon
Skin 'n' blister – sister
Sky rocket – pocket

Slap 'n' tickle – pickle
Smash 'n' grab – cab, taxi
Sorry 'n' sad – bad
Spanish onion – bunion
Spike – workhouse
Spitalfields breakfast – no breakfast, a reference to the poverty in the area
Spondoolies – money
Stewed prune – tune
Sticky toffee – coffee
Strawberry tart – heart
Stutter 'n' stammer – hammer
Sugar 'n' spice – ice
Swear 'n' cuss – bus
Sweeney Todd – Flying Squad – a division of the London police dealing with armed robbery
Syrup of fig – wig

T

Tate 'n' Lyle – style
Taters in the mould – cold – means potatoes in the ground and is abbreviated to **'taters'**
Tea leaf – thief
Tea 'n' toast – post
Teapot lids – kids

Tenner – ten-pound note

These 'n' those – toes

This 'n' that – cat

Three blind mice – rice

Tick-tock – clock

Tiddlywink – alcoholic drink

Tilbury Docks – pox

Tile – hat

Tina Turner – earner

Tin of fruit – suit

Tin tack – sack

Tit for tat – hat – abbreviation is **'titfer'**

Toby jug – lug, ear

Todd Sloane – alone

Tom 'n' Dick – sick

Tomfoolery – jewellery – often shortened to 'tom'

Tom Hanks – thanks

Tom Mix – six – Tom Mix was a star of many early American Western films

Tommy Tucker – supper

Tom Thumb – rum

Ton – £100

Tooting Beck – peck, as in food, but also peck meaning kiss

Tooting Beckish – peckish

Trafalgar Square – chair

Treacle tart – sweetheart
Treble chance – dance
Trolley 'n' tram – ham
Trouble 'n' fuss – bus
Trouble 'n' strife – wife
Turtle doves – gloves
Two 'n' eight – an emotional state
Two-thirty – dirty
Tuppence – two old pennies
Tyburn jig, to dance the – to be hanged, executed

U, V

Ugly sister – blister
Uncle Reg – veg, vegetables
Vera Lynn – gin

W, X, Y, Z

Watch 'n' chain – brain
Weasel 'n' stoat – coat
Wedge – money, usually notes
Weeping willow – pillow
Westminster Abbey – cabbie, taxi driver
Whale 'n' gale – out of jail
Whip 'n' lash – moustache

Whistle 'n' flute – suit

White mice – ice

Widow Twanky – hanky, handkerchief

William Tell – smell

Wind 'n' kite – website

Wobbly jelly – telly, television

Woolwich ferry – sherry

Working classes – glasses

Wotcher – a greeting – a corruption of 'what cheer'

Wunner – £100

Poplar Scooter Club, 1936

Cockney Counting

One – penny bun

Two – me and you

Three – trey, Vicar of Bray

Four – knock on the door

Five – beehive

Six – chopsticks

Seven – gates of heaven

Eight – garden gate

Nine – mother of mine

Ten – Bill 'n' Ben

"Forty fahzen fevvers on a frush"

Practise this to achieve the Cockney pronunciation *'th'* as *'f'*.

Oranges and lemons

The church bells of London all had their own unique sound and the rhyme for each of the bells would have matched their peals.

Oranges and Lemons,
Say the bells of St Clement's.
You owe me five farthings,
Say the bells of St Martin's.

When will you pay me?
Say the bells of Old Bailey.
When I grow rich,
Say the bells of Shoreditch.

When will that be?
Say the bells of Stepney.
I do not know,
Says the great bell at Bow.

In an older version of 'Oranges and Lemons' it also mentions:

Two sticks and apple,
Ring ye bells o' Whitechapel,
Old Father Bald Pate,
Ring ye bells at Aldgate.

Either St Clement Danes or St Clement Eastcheap is likely to be the one mentioned in this nursery rhyme as they are both near the old Thames Street wharves where ships from the Mediterranean unloaded their oranges and lemons. The 'owing of five farthings' may refer to the money-lending district around St Martin's Lane in the City and if the request for payment by the bells of Old Bailey was not forthcoming, Fleet Prison for debtors was nearby. The 'great bell at Bow' appears to refer to the church at St Mary-le-Bow in Cheapside, the same bells that rang out 'Turn again' to Dick Whittington (c.1350–1425). In the pantomime story Dick is depicted as very poor and, on despairing of making a fortune in London, he decides to leave the city. All of a sudden, he hears the bells of Bow call out 'Turn again, Whittington, Lord Mayor of London.' He duly turns round and finds he has made his fortune and is appointed Lord Mayor of London!

The real Dick Whittington was a wealthy merchant, importing and exporting luxury fabrics such as silk, linen and woollen cloth and was a supplier to the Royal Courts of Richard II, Henry IV and Henry V. He was elected alderman of Lime Street and then appointed Mayor of London in 1397. As well as endowing a library, public lavatories and almshouses, he gave money to build a refuge for unmarried mothers at St Thomas's Hospital, and when he died he left his entire fortune to charity.

Ice Cream Vendor, Grundy Street, 1930

Pop goes the Weasel

Half a pound of tuppenny rice
Half a pound of treacle,
Mix it up and make it nice,
Pop goes the weasel.

Up and down the City Road,
In and out the Eagle,
That's the way the money goes,
Pop goes the weasel.

31

One of the explanations of this rhyme is that a weasel (weasel 'n' stoat) is a coat and to 'pop the weasel' is to pawn it – usually on a Monday, so as to get it back for the weekend. The Eagle is likely to be the Eagle Tavern and Grecian Theatre with Pleasure Gardens which stood on the corner of City Road and Shepherdess Place from 1825. Entertainments included wrestling, equestrian acts, freak shows, clowns, dramas and concerts. It was a very popular venue, attracting thousands of people. The music hall singer Marie Lloyd's father was a part-time waiter there and she was only fourteen when she first performed at the Grecian Theatre. Her real name was Matilda Alice Victoria Wood (1870–1922) and she was a sensation with her glamorous gowns, a voice with perfect pitch and her performances, littered with innuendo and bawdy ad-libs. She sang 'The Boy I Love is up in the Gallery' at the Star Palace of Varieties in Bermondsey and it soon became her theme tune. By 1886 she was earning £100 a week, a fortune in those days. The Eagle was bought by the Salvation Army in 1883 and demolished in 1901.

Children queuing for Farthing Bundles at Fern Street, c.1920

Farthing Bundles

Clara Ellen Grant was the head teacher of a new school in Fern Street which opened in 1907. She was determined that her school would care for the welfare of the children and their families as well as educating them. As no child can learn when they are starving, she provided cheap school breakfasts, lunches and evening meals and Fern Street was the first school in London to run a clinic for its pupils. She set up a settlement where mothers were paid a wage for making clothes that could be sold locally at a reasonable price. Profits from this enterprise allowed

Clara to sell essential items cheaply through her clubs as she did not believe in just giving them away. There were boot clubs, coal clubs, clubs for fireguards and many other items. When people heard of the work being done by Clara and her volunteers, they generously sent clothing, toys and a variety of odds and ends. The small items were made up into bundles, wrapped in newspaper and sold on Saturday mornings for a farthing (a quarter of an old penny). The farthing bundles were very popular and there were great long queues of boys one week and girls the next. A wooden arch was made and only children who could walk under it were allowed to buy a farthing bundle, full of surprises. The sign on the arch said 'Enter all ye children small, None can come who are too tall.'

Jellied Eel Seller at Sclater Street Market, 1956

Jellied Eels

Jellied eels are a traditional dish from the East End, where eels were easily available as they were caught locally. The eels are boiled or stewed with herbs, and when cooled, the liquid turns to jelly. They are served with a green parsley sauce called 'liquor' and mashed potatoes. Tubby Isaac's Jellied Eel Stall is still in Goulston Street, outside the Aldgate Exchange Pub, just around the corner from Aldgate station. Here you can buy a variety of seafood as well as jellied eels. Although Tubby and his sons dashed off to America in 1939, just before the Second World War, the stall was taken over by his nephew and it has remained in the family ever since.

Tubby Isaac's Jellied Eels Stall, 2013

Pie 'n' Mash

Originally, these were fish pies, stuffed with cooked eels and served with 'liquor'. Later the pies were made from scraps of meat and vegetables or leftovers, covered with pastry and served with mashed potatoes, liberally covered with 'liquor'. Nowadays, minced beef is mostly used, along with onions, mushrooms and ale. The very thing to serve at your next 'knees up'!

Fish 'n' Chips

The East End is said to be the first place in England to have a fish 'n' chip shop. It was opened in 1860, in Cleveland Street, by Joseph Mallin, a Jew from Eastern Europe. During the First and Second World Wars, fish 'n' chips were not rationed as they were a staple diet for munitions workers and poorer families.

It is said that British troops identified each other during the D-Day landings by calling out 'fish' and expecting the response 'chips'. Any other response and they would have had their chips!

Beigel Seller in Stepney, 1938

Beigel, *pronounced 'buy-gall'*

These round rolls with a hole in the middle, crisp on the outside and chewy on the inside, where introduced to the East End by the Jews. Traditional beigels are made with yeast dough and boiled or steamed before baking. The Beigel Shop at 155 Brick Lane was established in 1855. At number 159 is the Beigel Bake, Brick Lane Bakery, where millions of beigels are baked every year as well as different varieties of bread, pastries and cakes (their apple strudel is delicious). The bakery is open 24/7 and favourite beigel fillings include hot salt beef and smoked salmon with cream cheese.

Ruby Murray

Curry gained popularity in the East End after many Bangladeshis arrived looking for work in the 1950s and 60s. The Spitalfields area, which used to be mainly occupied by the Jewish families, became home to Bangladeshis from Sylhet. As the number of tailors' shops reduced, the curry houses increased; they already had a good reputation for catering as, traditionally, the Bangladeshis had been cooks on board British ships. Nowadays, a wide variety of Ruby Murrays are available in fast food outlets along Whitechapel Road and in the restaurants around Brick Lane. With some of the street signs in Bengali script as well as English, this area has become known as Banglatown.

Brick Lane street sign in Bengali script

Famous East End Sweets

Do you remember Fruit Salad, your tongue turning black with the aniseed Black Jacks, lime and chocolate Double Agents, fizzy Refreshers, rolls of Fruit Pastilles, Pineapple Drops and Sherbet Fountains? Grocers Thomas King and Robert Robertson became partners with William Woodcock, a sugar boiler, in a sweet-making business, Robertson & Woodcock Ltd. Although Trebor is Robert spelt backwards, this was not the reason the company used it as their trademark. The site they rented on Shaftesbury Road was already called Trebor Works.

During the First World War, Trebor made a confectionery called 'Army and Navy Paregoric Tablets' which contained camphorated tincture of opium and, as might be expected, these were very popular with the forces. Their Extra Strong Mints, still well known today, were first made in the 1930s. However, work in the sweet factory was not without its dangers; sometimes the icing sugar contained drift metal and now and then a spark would cause an explosion.

Although sweets were rationed from July 1942 until 1953, Wrapped Fruit Drops, containing ascorbic acid (Vitamin C), were ordered by the ton by the American Armed Forces. Fruit Drops were also parachuted down to Chindit troops who were fighting the Japanese in the Burmese jungle. In 1944, the factory suffered bomb damage along with a row of shops and houses across the street. After the War, the East End factory was working to capacity, so a new factory opened in Ilford and this is where the fruit-flavoured 'Refreshers' were made. Trebor became part of Cadbury Schweppes in November 1989.

M. J. Cornbleet Grocery Shop, 1955

Cup of Rosy, luv? There's nothing like a pair of kippers and a cup of Rosy on the Cain 'n' Abel

The East India Company imported tea from China from the seventeenth century and clippers, like the Cutty Sark, landed their cargoes at Shad Thames and St Katherine's Dock. However, the Chinese were not interested in buying British goods so the ships lacked a full cargo for their return journey. Instead of paying for their tea with silver the East India Company secretly supplied the Chinese with opium, grown in Bengal. The Chinese authorities were determined to stop this import as it ruined the lives of their people, who became opium addicts. In retaliation, the British Government and the East India Company waged war on China. The Chinese were defeated in the two Opium Wars and they were forced to allow trade at five treaty ports, with Hong Kong being leased to Britain until 1997.

East India Docks, 1950

In these unsettled times, the East India Company was desperate to increase tea supplies from India, but the tea quality was not so good and they did not know how to produce green tea. The Scotsman, Robert Fortune (1812–1880), once curator of London's Chelsea Physic Garden, was a botanist, plant hunter, author, adventurer and industrial spy – the very person the Company needed to discover the secrets of Chinese tea production and to ship plants and seeds to the Indian plantations. Fortune, who was familiar with travelling in China dressed as a Chinese man, complete with wig and ponytail, took up the challenge on behalf of the East India Company. Tea seeds (Camellia sinensis) quickly become unviable and plants carried on the decks of ships died when sprayed with salty sea water and were easily washed overboard in bad weather. Fortune had already solved these problems when bringing back plants from China for the Royal Horticultural Society by using special wooden cases with glass sides, a bit like a triangular cold frame. These were designed by Whitechapel's Nathaniel Ward (1791–1868) and have become known as Wardian cases. The cases protected the plants and allowed seeds to germinate en route. Fortune successfully shipped 1,700 germinating seeds and 2,000 tea plants to Calcutta in 1851.

This was not enough for the East India Company as they were desperate to discover the secret of green tea production. Fortune, again dressed in Chinese costume, spied on the Chinese production methods and discovered it was the process and not the plant that produced green tea. Using his persuasive abilities, he also recruited Chinese tea workers for the Indian plantations. Fortune was a prolific plant hunter and introduced hundreds of plants to British gardens including the Chusan Palm (Trachycarpus fortunei) and the Kumquat (Fortunella japonica). London dominated the world tea trade and by 1890, the supplies came mostly from India.

Thomas Twining

Thomas Twining worked for the East India Company before setting up his own business selling the finest teas.

Twinings Shop and Museum, 216 Strand, 2013

Twining's original shop, established in 1706, is at 216 Strand, where you can still buy Twinings tea and visit their very small but interesting tea museum.

Crimps

The East End became home to itinerant seamen, including the Lascar crewmen from the East India Company, who were highly regarded by British ship owners as good workers and also, perhaps, because they were only paid one-fifth of a British sailor's wage. Irish, Jewish, Scottish, Dutch and Scandinavian seamen as well as ex-slaves from the Caribbean made this a cosmopolitan area. Around the docks devious men known as crimps preyed on these sea-goers by tricking them out of their wages, getting them drunk and then selling them to ships as crew.

Chinatown

Over the years, Chinese sailors made up a small community in Limehouse with laundries, restaurants and opium dens, turning this dockside area into London's first Chinatown. Ming, Pekin, Nankin and Canton are still names of streets here. During the Second World War, Limehouse was extensively damaged and then demolished. A new Chinatown was established in Soho.

West India Import Dock, 1892

Statue of Robert Milligan (1746–1809), a wealthy West Indies merchant and ship owner whose family had sugar plantations in Jamaica. He was instrumental in the planning and building of the West India Docks, which were officially opened in 1802.

The warehouses at West India Quay were built to store sugar, coffee and rum. The heavier imports such as sugar would be stored on the lower floors and lighter imports like coffee on the upper floors.

RUM & SUGAR

West India Docks

Gallons of rum, vast quantities of sugar, indigo dye, rubber, coffee, dates, spices, tobacco and tea were all unloaded from the ships at the West India Import Dock. The docks were also part of the Slave Triangle Trade, and from when they opened in 1802 until the abolition of the slave trade in Britain in 1807, seventy-seven ships left for West Africa where they purchased 24,962 enslaved Africans who were then transported to the Americas for sale. Over three thousand of these enslaved people died during the journey.

The docks closed in the 1980s and is now called West India Quays, with its own Docklands Light Railway station. The Museum of London Docklands occupies a two-hundred-year-old warehouse here and the north quay of the West India Export Dock is now Canary Wharf.

Speakin' proppa

'Yer know that young feller as come ter stay in our 'ouse six months ago? Well, w'en furst 'e come, I give yer my word, 'e didn't know nofink but 'is own language. We bin learnin' 'im English an' now 'e can speak it proppa – jes the same as wot you an' me can!'

Wickham's Department Store, Mile End Road, c.1950

The 'arrods of the East: Wickham's Department Store

Thomas Wickham expanded his drapery shop by buying up properties along the Mile End Road and eventually had a complete row, apart from the jewellery shop at number 81, owned by the Spieglhalter family, who would not sell their premises under any circumstances. In the end, Wickham's department store, which opened in 1927, was built around it. Wickham's closed in the 1960s and they never achieved their dream of a continuous frontage.

Gardiner's Corner: Gateway to the East End

Gardiner's Corner, 1959

Gardiner & Company's clothing store stood on the busy and perhaps hazardous junction of Commercial Road and Whitechapel High Street, as emblazoned across the corner was a sign urging 'Make Stepney Mean Safety'. High above this was a huge advertisement for Capstan cigarettes by W. D. & H. O. Wills. This was well sited as the store sold clothing for seamen and naval uniforms adorned their windows. The clock tower fell down when the building was gutted by fire not long after the store closed in the 1970s. As part of the regeneration of Aldgate new skyscrapers are now being built around here.

Pearly Kings and Queens

In the eighteenth century the costermongers from each borough elected a Coster King or Queen to represent them and fight for their rights. These had to be outspoken and quick-witted people with strong personalities and their children became Coster Princes and Princesses. Their secret language was Coster backslang, which was used to confuse their customers and the authorities. Eventually Cockney rhyming slang was also used for this purpose. In the nineteenth century, when pearls were fashionable with upper-class Londoners, the Coster Kings and Queens sewed flashes of cheap pearl buttons on their old waistcoats, caps and trousers.

Their costumes became more elaborate after Pearly King Henry Croft incorporated patterns, symbols and words into his designs in the 1880s. As well as fighting for the rights of their communities, they raised money to look after the poor and helped them in a good-hearted manner, without pity or condescension. Today the Pearly Kings and Queens are generous fundraisers for charities.

Brick Lane Market, 1968

Kool, the escilop!

Coster backslang is saying words backwards, making it a sort of secret code between those in the know. Some words could not be spoken backwards without adding an extra vowel or changing letters to make them pronounceable, as in old which becomes delo, and police and penny which become escilop and yennep. This backslang was used by costermongers before Cockney rhyming slang became popular. Henry Mayhew, writing in the 1860s, says that a costermonger told him, 'The Irish can't tumble to it anyhow; the Jews can tumble better . . . The police don't understand us at all. It would be a pity if they did.'

Here are a few useful phrases:

Flatchkanurd – half drunk

Kool the escilop! – Look, the police!

On doog – no good

Top 'o' reeb – pot of beer

Flatch – halfpenny

Yennep – penny

Ewif-yennep – fivepence

Net-yenep – tenpence

In France there is a similar slang called Verlan. The difference is that the syllables are reversed and not the words, making café into féca and bonjour into jourbon.

'My uncle had a butcher's shop and they spoke backslang amongst themselves so that they could pass the customer off with some old meat without them knowing what was being said!'

'Back-slang was spoken in families and the children picked it up. Some people I worked with spoke it but I could never understand it.'

Club Row Market, Bird Seller, 1956

Awright, geezza cherry 'og 'n' a ball of fat, me ol' China

Fer donkey's ears, the Sunday Club Row Market did a roarin' trade in pets and the field of wheat was full of customers taking a butcher's at the cherry 'ogs and balls of fat as well as the hedge 'n' ditches selling collars and leads. Monkeys and parrots from far-off lands, rabbits, songbirds and pigeons, all for sale if you had some bangers 'n' mash in your sky rocket.

The most admired songbirds were linnets and canaries, for as well as bringing silk weaving to Spitalfields, the Huguenots brought their love of caged songbirds.

Fred W. Leigh and **Charles Collins'** old music hall favourite
'My Old Man' conjures up the scene of the trouble 'n'
strife walking along carrying her songbird in a cage.

> *My old man said follow the van,*
> *And don't dilly dally on the way,*
> *Off went the van wiv me 'ome packed in it,*
> *I followed on with my old cock linnet . . .*

Billingsgate market was the place for a bit of Lillian Gish, full
of hustle and bustle with costers shouting out 'Ha-a-ansome
cod! Best in the market. 'All alive, alive, alive O! Here's your
fine bloaters!' 'Fine grizzling sprats, all large and no small!'
The oyster traders sold from their boats along the wharf and
this area was known as Oyster-street.

Bethnal Green: Brunham Estate Living room, 1939

The traders, all vying for custom, would holler, 'Who's for Alstons?' 'Who's for Bakers?' and, to attract attention, rattled the shells with their spades. 'New mackerel, new mackerel!' could be heard on a Sunday, as it was allowed to be sold by street vendors because it would not keep. Perhaps this is source of the expression 'holy mackerel'?

'Listen luv, all the East End folk have moved to Essex – Romford Market is where you'll find 'em, not Newham or Tower Hamlets.'

'The East End is always changing. My family came 'ere from Ireland, then lots of Jews moved into the area and then the Bangladeshis. Lots of folk only stay until they can afford to move to another part of London but some like me come back 'cos there's no place like it.'

Spitalfields Market, 1912

Tricks of the Trade and Tossing the Pieman

Here are a couple of costermonger tricks of the trade from the nineteenth century.

Boiling oranges for a few minutes, thirty or forty at a time, swells them up and makes them look bigger and they can be sold for a higher price when trade is brisk on a Saturday and Sunday. After forty-eight hours, the oranges turn dark and are worthless.

Cheap red-skinned apples (gawfs) were mixed with better-quality apples. First the cheap apples must be rubbed with a woollen cloth or rolled in the palms of the hand to make them shiny and the skins feel soft. Smaller apples were put in a sack and two boys, each taking an end, would roll them backwards and forwards, making them shiny and appealing.

At the public houses a few pies are sold, and the pieman makes a practice of 'looking in' at all the taverns on his way. Here his customers are found, principally in the tap-room. "'ere's all 'ot!" the pieman cries as he walks into the taverns. "Toss or buy! Up an' win 'em!" This is the only way pies can be got rid of. "If it wasn't for tossing we shouldn't sell one."

To toss the pieman is a favourite pastime with

costermongers' boys. If the pieman wins the toss, he receives a penny (1d) without giving a pie; if he loses, he hands it over for nothing. The pieman himself never tosses but always calls head or tails to the customer. At the week's end it comes to the same thing, they say, whether they win or lose the toss. 'I've taken as much as 2/6d at tossing, which I shouldn't 'ave 'ad if I 'ad not done so. Very few people buy without tossing, the boys in particular. Gentlemen out on the spree at the late public houses will frequently toss when they don't want the pies and when they win, will amuse themselves by throwing the pies at one another or at me. The boys 'as the greatest love of gamblin' and they seldom, if every, buys without tossing.'

The 'gravy' which used to be given with the meat pies was poured out of an oil-can, and consisted of a little salt and water browned. A hole was made with the little finger in the pie and the gravy was poured in until the crust rose. With this gravy pies of four days old go off very freely and are pronounced excellent.

(Abridged from *London Labour and the London Poor* by Henry Mayhew, 1860–1861)

Workers going home from Bryant and May's Match Factory, 1910

Safety Cuts 'n' Scratches

Cuts 'n' scratches (matches) were discovered by mistake in 1827 when John Walker rubbed a stick on a rough surface and it burst into flames. He had been using this stick to mix potassium chlorate, antimony sulphide and gum-Arabic. These matches were not safe as just leaving the box in sunshine could cause them to ignite. Friction matches soon became one of life's essentials and match sellers were frequently seen around the docks and markets.

William Bryant (1804–1874) was a manufacturer of blacking, candles and lubricants and Francis May (1803–1885) was a tea merchant and grocer at 20 Bishopsgate. They became partners in 1843 and traded as provision merchants. By 1850, most of the matches sold in Britain were manufactured abroad and they bought matches from the Swedes, Carl and Johan Lundström, who bought large quantities of uncut wax taper from them. Johan discovered that by including chlorate of potash in the match-head mixture, and adding amorphous phosphorus to the grit solution that was painted on the boxes, the matches were much safer. Bryant and May bought the patent rights to these new safety matches in 1852, but they continued to buy their supplies from Sweden. However, supplies were erratic and insufficient so in 1860 Bryant and May acquired a three-acre site in Fairfield Road in Bow and their new factory, designed by Lundström, was built to manufacture 'patent safety matches and other chemical lights'. Shortly afterwards Bryant's son Wilberforce (1837–1906) joined the company as factory manager. Francis May left the company in 1875.

Women and children were employed to made matchboxes at home and paid tuppence for making 144. Although the factory initially used the safe red phosphorus, they could not compete on price, so made matches with the cheaper white phosphorus, which caused 'phossy jaw'. The matchmakers were not happy with their working conditions or about being laid off in the summer when sales dropped. Annie Besant, the Fabian Society reformer, wrote an article titled 'White Slavery in London' and the matchgirls who had spoken to Annie were sacked. This resulted in a three-week strike. They returned to slightly better conditions but white phosphorous continued to be used. By 1897 Bryant and May employed about two thousand matchgirls. Eventually, machines were brought in to dip the splints and the firm employed a doctor and dentist to look out for early signs of cancer of the jaw.

Phossy Jaw

Phossy Jaw is caused by the fumes of white phosphorus penetrating the jawbone through cavities in decaying teeth. The matchgirls would suffer from toothache, swelling of the gums and abscesses on the jawbone, which would glow in the dark. The rotting of the dying bone tissue caused a foul-smelling discharge and the face became badly disfigured. In later stages, it caused brain damage and death from organ failure. The Salvation Army knew that red phosphorus would not cause phossy jaw, so they opened their own match factory in Bow in 1891, paying workers a fair wage. However, these safer matches cost three times the price of the white phosphorous matches and they struggled to sell them in sufficient numbers. Their factory closed and Bryant and May took it over in 1901. White phosphorus continued to be used in Britain until it was banned by an Act of Parliament in 1910.

Diagnosis

Doctor: *'I can tell you what you are suffering from, my good chap. You're suffering from acne.'*

Patient: *''ackney? Why that's just what the last Doc told me! I wish I'd never been near the place.'*

Fast Sausage 'n' Mash

If you only 'ave goose's necks, you might need to sausage a goose's. Don't forget your Huckleberry Finn if you're using a cash machine. According to the Docklands Museum there are about thirty ATMs in the East End that offer Cockney as an alternative language. The instructions include 'Take your bladder of lard. Sausage and mash will follow.'

Money – bread, dough, poppy, moolah

Small change – mouldies

Bet – jumbo jet, house to let

Penny – Abergavenny

£1 – lost 'n' found, quid, bin lid, knicker, Alan Whicker

£5 – beehive, fiver, deep sea diver, Lady Godiva

£10 – cock 'n' hen, speckled hen, tenner, Bill 'n'Benner,

£15 – Commodore – as the Commodores sang
'Three Times a Lady' and three Lady Godivas equals £15

£20 – horn of plenty, score, apple core

£25 – pony, macaroni

£30 – dirty

£40 – double top

£50 – bull's eye, nifty

£100 – ton, wunner, bill

£500 – monkey

£1,000 – grand, bag of sand

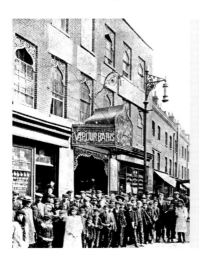

Schewik's Russian Vapour Baths, 86 Brick Lane, c. 1920.

They advertised 'the best massage in London' and declared that the baths gave 'Invaluable Relief for Rheumatism, Gout, Sciatica, Neuritis, Lumbago and allied complaints'

Was it Royal Mail and no jam roll for these Joe Hooks?

Dick Turpin *(c.1705–1739)*

Dick was a butcher's apprentice in Whitechapel and supplemented his earnings as a Joe Hook. He moved to Essex and stocked his butcher's shop with half-inched meat. He was a house burglar, a smuggler, a highwayman, a horse thief and a murderer. He half-inched a racehorse which ended up in a stable behind the Red Lion rub-a-dub in Whitechapel. Dick, inadvertently, shot brown bread his partner in crime and then managed to escape. Eventually, he was caught, sentenced and danced the Tyburn jig outside the walls of York. His life was romanticised in Harrison Ainsworth's novel *Rookwood (1834)*.

Jack the Ripper

During the summer and autumn of 1888, horrific murders were committed in Whitechapel. The Central News Agency received a letter, written in red ink, supposedly from the perpetrator, and signed 'Jack the Ripper'. Many of the victims, said to be prostitutes, were cruelly mutilated, some had their organs removed with precision and others were stabbed many times in what could be described as a frenzied attack. The victims included Mary Ann Nichols, Annie Chapman, Elizabeth Stride, Catherine Eddowes and Mary Kelly. To this day no one knows for certain the identity of this cruel, vicious murderer.

Blind Beggar Pub, Mile End Road, 2013

The Kray Twins of the East End

Reggie *(1933–2000)* and **Ronnie** *(1933–1995)* **Kray** were twins, born in Hoxton and brought up at 178 Vallance Road in Bethnal Green. Their father, Charles, was absent much of the time but their grandfathers, Cannonball Lee and Mad Jimmy Kray, had an influence in their upbringing. During the Second World War, they were evacuated to Suffolk with their elder brother, Charles, who trained them to box, and they both achieved professional boxer status by the time

64

they were seventeen. Reggie and Ronnie had a reputation for violence and their main sources of income appears to have come from extortion, protection and illegal gambling.

The twins were called up for national service in 1952 and, after spending much of their time in military prisons, they were both dishonourably discharged after fifteen months. In 1955, Ronnie, armed with a cutlass, scattered a gang who tried to take over a billiard hall that the twins were protecting in the Mile End Road.

Their base was the Double R Club in Bow Road and after it lost its licence their operation moved to the Kentucky on the Mile End Road. The twins socialised with Members of Parliament and show-business celebrities including Judy Garland, Barbara Windsor, Diana Dors and Frank Sinatra. Their portraits were taken by photographer David Bailey, also from the East End.

In 1965, Reggie married Frances Shea and was devastated when she committed suicide in 1967. Ronnie shot dead George Cornell in the Blind Beggar pub on the Mile End Road in 1966, but no one was willing to identify him. A year later, Reggie stabbed and killed Jack 'the Hat' McVitie. The Krays were convicted of these murders at their trial at the Old Bailey in 1969, and sentenced to life imprisonment, with a recommendation that they serve at least thirty years.

Ronnie, who was diagnosed with paranoid schizophrenia, was moved to Broadmoor high-security psychiatric hospital in 1979. While in prison, Ronnie first married Elaine Mildiner in 1985 and, after they were divorced, he married Kate Howard, divorcing her the year before he died of a heart attack in 1995. Reggie married Roberta Rachael Jones in 1997 while he was serving his sentence. He was released on compassionate grounds in September 2000 when suffering from terminal cancer and died shortly afterwards. Their elder brother Charles was imprisoned in 1996 for supplying drugs and promising to supply cocaine with a value of £39 million. He died in prison in 2000.

Sophie Tucker at the Rivoli Cinema, Mile End Road, c.1920

Have a good ol' knees up and a ding-dong

Any Ol' Iron

Any ol' iron? Any ol' iron?

Any, any, any ol' iron?

You look neat. Talk about a treat,

Looking so dapper from your napper to your feet.

Dressed in style, brand new tile,

And your father's old green tie on,

But I wouldn't give you tuppence for your ol' fob watch

Ol' iron, ol' iron.

(by Collins, Terry and Sheppard, 1911)

Lambeth Walk

This popular Cockney song was written by Noel Gay for the 1937 musical "Me and My Girl" by Douglas Furber and Arthur Rose. Lupino Lane popularised the dance where couples link arms and stride forwards and then backwards, and, at the end of the verse, give a thumbs-up sign and shout 'Oi!'

Any time you're Lambeth way,

Any evening, any day,

You'll find us all,

Doing the Lambeth Walk.

Tate and Lyle and the Sugar Mile

With Abram Lyle & Sons at one end and Henry Tate & Sons at the other, and with James Keiller & Sons, jam, marmalade and confectionery manufacturers, in between, this was certainly a Sugar Mile. The Tate's new Thames Refinery opened in Silvertown in 1878, on the site of a derelict shipyard; an ideal spot for unloading raw sugar. Instead of making sugar loaves, which had to be cut up before use, they manufactured sugar cubes. About a mile upstream, at Plaistow Wharf, Lyle began production of Golden Syrup in 1883 and two years later it was packaged in the distinctive gold and green tin, still in use today. They had a gentlemen's agreement that Lyle would not make sugar cubes and Tate would not make syrup. In 1921 they

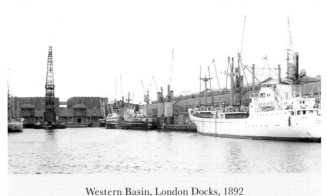

Western Basin, London Docks, 1892

refined about half of the country's sugar. The workers were mainly young girls and women who, after making a few stylish alterations, were proud of their uniforms. Wages were the best in the area and there was a profit-sharing scheme, a company doctor, chiropodist, hairdresser and sports facilities, as well as a bar and social club at the Tate Institute. The company even paid for sick workers to convalesce by the sea. As well as manufacturing the products, cans were made for the golden syrup and sugar bags printed, filled, sealed and packed on pallets. The company organised beanos (workers' outings) to Southend and Margate. The Tate & Lyle Times kept everyone up to date with news about the business and the workers' sporting achievements. It was an honour for a sugar girl to be chosen to promote the company at the Ideal Home Exhibition in London.

In 2012, Tate & Lyle sold its sugar businesses, including the Lyle's Golden Syrup brand, to American Sugar Refining, Inc. and licensed them to use the 'Tate & Lyle Sugar' name. Sir Henry Tate (1819–1899) endowed a new art gallery, now called Tate Britain, which opened in 1897. If you are interested in finding out what it was like working in the Blue Room or operating the Hesser machines, read *The Sugar Girls, Tales of Hardship, Love and Happiness* by Duncan Barrett and Nuala Calvi (Collins, 2012).

Tottie

Written by **G. R. Sims** *(1847–1922)*, this song was published
in *The Referee* in 1887.

As she walked along the street,
With her little plates of meat,
And the summer sunshine falling
On her golden Barnet Fair.
Bright as angels from the skies
Were her dark blue mutton pies.
In my East and West Dan Cupid
Shot a shaft and left it there.
Sh'd a Grecian I suppose
And of Hampstead Heath two rows,
In her sunny south that glistened
Like two pretty strings of pearls;
Down on my bread and cheese
Did I drop and murmur, 'Please
Be my storm and strife, dear Tottie,
O, you darlingest of girls!'

Hat 'n' Feather Forecast

'Today the Bath Bun will shine over the East End but
there may be some Rawalpindi days next week. In the
gypsy's warning there may be some Frarny but no buck 'n'
doe or white mice.'

The Great Smog of 1952

Smog was nothing new to London, but with the increase in pollution, industries and coal fires, this was a particularly bad year and for four days in December 1952 everything ground to a halt. This poisonous smog was a fog laced with sulphur dioxide, nitrogen oxides and soot, caused by pollution and the extreme cold. The worst-affected part of London was the East End as it is was low lying and had many factories and dense housing. This foul-smelling, choking, yellow smog spread everywhere, even into cinemas, making it nearly impossible to see the film or to hear it with all the coughing. Buses and trams tried to keep going as long as possible with the clippies, as well as the drivers, keeping a lookout to make sure they did not bump into something or someone. On the Isle of Dogs, it was so bad people could not see as far as their feet! During the Great Smog over four thousand people died from respiratory or cardiovascular problems. The 1956 and 1968 Clean Air Acts banned emissions of black smoke, and homes and factories had to convert to smokeless fuel.

Cholera and the Great Pen 'n' Ink

'The pen was so bad cloths were soaked in chloride and lime and hung on the windows of Parliament but they did nought to stop the Judi.'

In 1832 the area around the docks was struck by an outbreak of cholera and the cause was thought to be a miasma or bad smell. Limehouse, Shadwell, Whitechapel and Bethnal Green used parts of their workhouses to care for cholera victims as the London Hospital would not accept them. The first patient to arrive at the Limehouse workhouse was Sarah Ferguson, who turned blue shortly before dying just a few hours later, confirming the diagnosis of the dreadful 'Asiatic' cholera. Hundreds of people died in the East End alone during this outbreak and in 1848 the situation was much worse. The following year **Dr John Snow** discovered that cholera was transmitted through water and it was only then that the connection between polluted drinking water and the disease was made.

Despite the Thames being the main source of drinking water, sewage and effluent from houses, factories and chemical works poured into the river. In 1858 Parliament stopped sitting due to the stink and in the end the government had to take action and tackle the root cause of the problem.

Joseph Bazalgette *(1819–1891)*, an engineer, was given the go-ahead to build the London sewage system but this was no overnight solution. The embankments also had to house the new Underground lines so the work took some time to complete. Sadly another cholera epidemic hit the East End in 1866, as they were not yet connected to the sewage system. This time public information was circulated telling everyone to boil all drinking water.

Famous Locals

William Addis *(d.1808)* invented a toothbrush while in Newgate Gaol in 1780. When released he made some more brushes from animal bones and horsehair and had them manufactured in the homes of pieceworkers in Spitalfields and Whitechapel. Eventually, the Addis Company marketed its products as Wisdom Toothbrushes and produced their first nylon toothbrushes in the 1940s. The Addis family ran the company until 1996.

Doctor Thomas John Barnardo *(1845–1905)* began his work with children at 58 Solent House, Ben Jonson Road in Stepney. When he came to the East End he found children sleeping in the streets and begging for food. To help these vulnerable and neglected children he set up the Ragged School to educate and care for them. The Ragged School Museum is in Copperfield Road, near Mile End Park.

William Booth *(1829–1912)* formed the Salvation Army at a meeting in Whitechapel Road in 1878.

Sir Thomas Fowell Buxton *(1786–1845)*, the anti-slavery campaigner, lived at and worked from The Directors' House, Old Truman Brewery, 91 Brick Lane.

William Booth's Statue
in Whitechapel Road

Edith Cavell *(1865–1915)*, a pioneer of modern nursing, trained and worked at the London Hospital, Whitechapel and was, for a time, assistant matron of Shoreditch Infirmary. During the First World War she helped Allied soldiers to escape from German-occupied Belgium and for this she was tried for treason and shot by a German firing squad in 1915.

Sir Jack Cohen *(1898–1979)*, the founder of Tesco, lived at 91 Ashfield Street in Whitechapel. When he was demobbed he bought surplus NAAFI foodstuffs and sold them from a market stall in Hackney.

Bud Flanagan *(1896–1968)*, born Chaim Reuben Weintrop and leader of the 'Crazy Gang', was born at 12 Hanbury Street, Spitalfields.

Charles Henry Harrod *(1799–1885)* opened his wholesale grocers and tea emporium at 4 Cable Street in 1834. His son **Henry Digby Harrod** *(1841–1905)* expanded the business and opened a new Harrods Department Store in Brompton Road in 1884.

Sylvia Pankhurst *(1882–1960)*, who lived in Bow for twelve years, set up the East London Federation of Suffragettes in 1913. Women over twenty-one were given the right to vote in 1928.

Explosions, Scares and Bombs

On 19 January 1917, in the evening, the East End was rocked by a massive explosion at the TNT factory in Silvertown. The Brunner, Mond & Co. Chemical Works had been forced by the government to turn their production from caustic soda to TNT for munitions, a highly unstable explosive. From 1915, nine tons of TNT was produced every day. The explosion instantly destroyed the factory as well as several streets nearby, starting fires that could be seen in Kent. Nine hundred homes were destroyed or damaged, making thousands of people homeless.

In the narrow streets of the East End many houses did not have gardens so very few Anderson Shelters were put up during the Second World War. Trench shelters were built in places like Victoria Park and Poplar Recreation Ground but these were poorly ventilated, waterlogged and strewn with litter so they were not used very much. People preferred the basement shelters like the ones at Bryant and May or Stephen Smith & Company, but these became overcrowded. An alternative was to shelter in a tube station.

About 10,000 people could squeeze into Bethnal Green Underground Station to shelter from the air raids. In 1943, a rocket-firing anti-aircraft battery was placed in Victoria Park but the local residents were not aware of this. On Wednesday 3 March, the first night these weapons were used, the unexpectedly loud noises panicked people

Approach road, Bethnal Green, 1941

who were on their way to the tube station at Bethnal Green. While descending the stairs to the platform one hundred and seventy-eight men, women and children were suffocated in the crush. A new memorial called the 'Stairway to Heaven' has been erected in their memory.

During the Second World War the East End suffered substantial damage from around fourteen hundred air raids along the Thames and the docks. About fifteen thousand high-explosive bombs were dropped as well as 550 flying bombs, 350 parachute mines and 240 rockets.

'When we was kids we played on the bomb sites. We 'ad names for them all like Black Panther and American Hole.'

Bomb damage in Hanbury Street and Spital Street, September 1940

You'd never Adam 'n' Eve it!

Pure Finders

In the late nineteenth century, pure finders collected dog's faeces (pure) from the streets and kennels and sold it by the bucketful to the tanneries in Bermondsey. Tanners of thin leathers such as calfskin mixed it with lime and bark to purify the skins. The leather-dressers rubbed this disgusting dog poo mixture into the skins using their bare hands. Dogs' poo is astringent and alkaline and it removes all the moisture from the leather.

Tosh

'Tosh' now means rubbish, as in 'Speaking a load of tosh.' It comes from boatmen, called toshers, who dredged the River Thames to keep it clear of flotsam and jetsam.

Mudlarks

These were mostly women and children who scavenged along the muddy banks of the Thames when the tide was out. They searched for treasures such as coal, iron rivets from ships, bits of wood, lumps of fat thrown overboard by ships' cooks and anything else they could use or sell. Sometimes the boys would sneak onto the coal barges and throw some coal into the river so that they could pick it up later. It was important to be a good swimmer because if the bargemen caught the mudlarks, they threw them overboard.

Millwall Football Team, 1894/95

Take a butcher's at this!

Millwall: Football 'n' Flour

Millwall Rovers football team was formed in 1885 by the workers from Morton's factory in West Ferry Road, where they produced jams and sweets. In 1910, the football club moved to South London.

Millwall Docks with its seven windmills was built to handle grain imported mostly from the Baltic. The first large mill was the Wheatsheaf, constructed in 1869 by the McDougall brothers, producers of the revolutionary self-raising flour. The grain workers in the warehouses were called toe-rags as they covered their boots with sacking.

Hop-pickers arriving
at London Bridge
Station, c.1920

Hopping

Mums and children from the East End would go off to Kent
hop-picking during the summer and their husbands would
sometimes join them at the weekends. Families would
spend the whole summer there, living in pickers' huts.
They took everything they needed with them, including
their bedding and cooking pots, and travelled to the hop
gardens on one of the special Hoppers' Trains. After the
Second World War, much of the picking was mechanised
and fewer summer workers were required.

Acknowledgements
I would like to thank the Museum of London Docklands, especially
Brian and Dave, and everyone who shared their memories of the
East End with me. A special thanks to Tower Hamlets Local History
Library and Archives for their permission to use photographs
from their archives and to Melanie Strong, their Heritage Officer.